Shared History

Shared History

Poems by

Jean L. Kreiling

Cover photograph of the Salisbury Crags,
Edinburgh, Scotland, by the author

ISBN: 978-1-63980-051-3

Kelsay Books
502 South 1040 East, A-119
American Fork, Utah 84003
Kelsaybooks.com

for my sisters and brother

Acknowledgments

I am grateful to the editors of the following publications, in which many of the poems in this book first appeared, some under different titles or in slightly different versions.

14 by 14: "The Waves"
Able Muse Review: "Waiting for the Helicopter," "The Watchers"
Autumn Sky Poetry Daily: "Living Room"
Coldnoon—Travel Poetics: "The English and Their Queen," "The Powell-Mason Cable Car," "On the Spanish Coast"
Contemporary Sonnet: "Well Fed"
Ekphrastic Review: "Hotel Room"
Extreme Sonnets (Rhizome Press): "When You Find Me Staring at the Ocean"
Fresh Ink: "The Runner"
Frostwriting: "The Salisbury Crags"
Innisfree Poetry Journal: "Faith," "On the Ferry Home," "Woman and Small Boy at the Beach"
Life and Legends: "Beethoven's Work Ethic"
Literary Matters: "Birdwatchers"
London Poetry Review: "My Grandmother and the Sea"
Long Island Quarterly: "Gloria's," "Luna's Pizza," "Sense of Direction," "Six Corners School," "Westhampton Free Library"
Lowestoft Chronicle: "Passport Control"
The Lyric: "Coastal Fog," "Sunrise at Sea"
Measure: "Hotel by a Railroad," "The Palette," "Sorting"
Mezzo Cammin: "Autumn Wish," "Family Reunion Photo Taken on a Cruise Ship," "Mirror Nonet for Three Sisters," "Old South Carriage Tour," "Where Everybody Knows Your Name"

Orchards Poetry Journal: "Memorial for Ben," "The Roaring"
Peacock Journal: "The Bourne Bridge, Late October"
Pennsylvania Review: "Flying Companion"
Poetrysocietyofvirginia.org: "Hotel Lobby"
The Road Not Taken: "Chess Players"
The Rotary Dial: "Harbor Walk"
Shot Glass Journal: "Same Model and Year, Different Speed"
Snakeskin: "Butch Cassidy and the Sundance Kid"
String Poet: "Inheritance"
Think: "The Tightrope Walker"

~~~

"Family Reunion Photo Taken on a Cruise Ship" was a Finalist in the Maria W. Faust Sonnet Contest.

"Hotel by a Railroad" and "Sorting" were Finalists for the Howard Nemerov Sonnet Award.

"Hotel Lobby" won Second Prize in the Elizabeth Neuwirth Memorial Poetry Competition, Poetry Society of Virginia.

"The Palette" won Honorable Mention for the Frost Prize (Robert Frost Foundation).

"The Runner" won the Great Lakes Commonwealth of Letters Sonnet Contest.

"Waiting for the Helicopter" won the *Able Muse* Write Prize.

Contents

III. Sea Sonnets

IV. Shared History

I
Persistence

"For us, there is only the trying.
The rest is not our business."
—T. S. Eliot, "East Coker"

The Palette

"Cold and the colors of cold . . .
I huddle, hoard, hold out, hold on, hold on."
—Robert Francis, "Cold"

The palette loses warmth: the hair gone gray,
the teeth not quite so white,
the skin spattered with spots—and not the spray

of tiny freckles firmer flesh might draw
from summer's genial light,
but larger, darker spots from glare as raw

as time itself. The ruthless artistry
of decades renders cold,
strange portraits of familiar atrophy.

Yet we assume that we can still resist,
still wield a brush and hold
an undiminished palette. We insist

we'll be preserved by grit and eloquence:
naïve as morning glories,
we clutch at canvases whose permanence

was never ours. We're victims of a con—
one made of our own stories,
and so persuasive we hold on, hold on.

Beethoven's Work Ethic

Italicized words and phrases come from the composer's "Heiligenstadt Testament," a letter written to his brothers concerning his deafness.

Betrayed by his own ears, he might have quit,
but conscience and his craft would not permit
surrender—he had work to do. A fierce,
broad face glares from the portraits: dark eyes pierce
our own as if in fury, and that mane
of unkempt hair must have been yanked in pain
and dread. At just past thirty, horrified
by weakness that he felt compelled to hide,
he mourned the fading of that faculty
once marked by its superiority
(*perfection* was his word), and thought of leaving
this earth. Retreating to the country, grieving
for unheard music, he at last despaired
of cures. But in the same breath he declared,
*It seemed to me impossible that I
should leave the world*—we almost hear him sigh—
*before I had brought forth all that I felt
was in me*. Praying for relief, he knelt
to *Providence*, and wondered if he'd know
real joy again. And so when we bestow
our praise on his quartets and symphonies—
produced despite his deepest agonies—
we're celebrating work that saved a man.
He'd labored on—a builder with a plan,
a farmer with a field to plow and seed,
a sailor with a sky of stars to read—
while duly worshipped gods took back the gift

he thought he needed most. Though cast adrift
in outer silence, Beethoven still heard
the waves inside, and wrote them, undeterred
by deafness. And it turned out that he needed
that perseverance most. Beethoven heeded
his own conviction that the world required
his *art*—the music so widely admired.
Asserting simply that he plied his trade
in earnest doesn't cheapen what he made,
but amplifies the nebulous acclaim
that calls him "genius." Few would doubt that name,
but we can also cite a plainer good,
a mortal virtue widely understood:
he worked hard. He used notes instead of nails,
reaped counterpoint instead of crops, trimmed sails
by stars that he discovered, and re-charted
old seas of newfound depth. Though broken-hearted,
he didn't break. Rejecting suicide,
embracing an ambition laced with pride
and obligation, Beethoven kept breathing
and working, writing hymns to joy while seething.
Of course his genius merits reverence—
but so does his uncommon diligence.

Five a.m. Sentries

Boxy bins on wheels line the pre-dawn curbside:
Wednesday morning soldiers at mute attention,
bearing someone else's detritus, brooking
       zero dissension.

They prefer this earliest pick-up hour,
atmospheric camouflage grimly keeping
grimy lids and uniforms darkly hidden
       while the world's sleeping.

Not quite proud, they're dutiful. They stand firm, though
sheepish, slightly mortified, blushing dark gray,
grateful for their cushy if dull assignment:
       guarding the driveway.

The Runner

for Kara

She runs the way she breathes, each muscle meant
for this, each stride more natural than rest,
her blond braid bobbing, her blue eyes intent,
legs effortlessly flexing in a test
of bone and sinew that she knows she'll ace
despite the pavement's punishing resistance,
arms pumping as if reaching to embrace
another mile, as lungfuls of persistence
propel her faster, farther. Someone eyes
a ticking stopwatch, ready to record
the minutes and the seconds as she flies
far past our earthbound selves—but her reward
consists of more than just a record time:
she runs to catch a breath of the sublime.

Living Room

after a painting by Alex Colville

His wife asked him to listen, so he does,
his straight-backed chair encouraging attention
as she plays Brahms. He can't say when it was
she last made this request; they hardly mention
their private interests to each other now,
so he's a little baffled. But he sits
respectfully, while marveling at how
the dog naps right through all the noisy bits,
snout pointed at the baby grand. Is this
the "living" called for by this room? This hour
of patient joylessness, this fear he'll miss
something that he should love? Brahms has no power
to move him. Though his wife plays earnestly,
the notes only confound him. So does she.

Two Paintings by Franz Borghese

I. *The Tightrope Walker (Il funambolo)*

The men below look up in fascination,
astounded by the walker's bravery.
Earthbound, their own steps marked by trepidation,
they envy him his poise and dignity.
But now, distracted by flapping blue wings,
the walker looks up, too, facing a threat
to balance, courage, and the other things
that he pretends to—and he has no net.
The only woman in the audience
does not look up, and she is not astounded.
She knows this daring act has precedents
in ordinary deeds, in lives as grounded
as her red shoes. It takes some grit, she knows,
to walk with grace, wherever your path goes.

II. *Chess Players (Giocatori di scacchi)*

He seldom sits this straight, but at this table
he mustn't yield a thing. And he won't blink
before she does. For her part, she's unable
to figure out what made her husband think
she might be beaten at this foolish game.
She's won at everything they've ever played—
although it's true she sometimes lets him claim
that he's the victor, part of a charade
to keep the peace. But she's all done with that;
from now on, she won't fake it. He, meanwhile,
is guessing that her perfectly straight hat
might tilt or fall if she should deign to smile.
He tries to focus. Both need this success,
both well aware they're not just playing chess.

Butch Cassidy and the Sundance Kid

after the 1969 film written by William Goldman and directed
by George Roy Hill

Two outlaws run, but never lose their cool;
they make their white-hat foe look like a fool.
Still handsome after their long, frantic ride,
our boys leap from a cliff—sure suicide
that they survive. While Sundance goes to school

in Etta's arms, Butch lets his wit unspool
on two wheels, unafraid of ridicule,
and three hearts laugh. But all that charm won't hide
two outlaws. Run

still farther—that's the desperadoes' rule.
Their chances of survival miniscule,
they try Bolivia, all three allied
in crime, but Etta leaves; she can't abide
the risks. At last, exposed by one damned mule,
two outlaws run.

Thank-You Note

"Nevertheless, she persisted."—Sen. Mitch McConnell, referring to Sen. Elizabeth Warren

I thank the women who resisted,
raised their voices and insisted,
marched, demanded, and persisted.

Faith

Dark robes, bright hopes, and words that live or die
according to the spirit that may move
or not move those who pray and don't ask why
they come each Sunday—all of this may prove
that faith survives. Or it may prove the force
of habit, or the galling rule of guilt,
or good behavior: kids learn not to horse
around in pews their parents' tithes have built.
Some people come here out of loneliness,
while others bow their heads in mortal fear.
One needs a place to wear a favorite dress;
another shows up every week to hear
the anthem. So the preacher does his best—
not always sure just whom or what he's blessed.

Sorting

She tips the plastic bottle, shakes out pills,
and places one in each compartment—"S,"
then "M," then "T"—pretending that her ills
will be subdued by drugs and tidiness.
Next come the oval tablets, two per day;
she counts out loud, believing in precision,
or trying to. She's troubled by the way
the tiny yellow ones challenge her vision
and her diminishing dexterity,
but manages those, too. If she can cope
with this routine, her son has to agree
to let her live at home. She dares to hope
that she'll count pills for years, appease her son,
and sort things out the way she's always done.

His Plan for Using the Walker

He'll grip the thing with authority—
the way he once gripped a putter,
the pen that inked the contracts,
his stumbling toddler's hand,
the wheel of the Ford,
his wife's wheelchair,
his scotch, neat.
He'll grip
this
clumsy
contraption
as if he knew
where he was going,
as if he were in charge,
as if he owned the outfit
that manufactured the fool thing,
as if he were free not to hold on.

Birdwatchers

I

Through panes of wavy glass, she glumly peers
at birds she knows. Though she can't say their names,
she's drawn by wings that swoop and songs she hears
through panes of wavy glass. She glumly peers
at feathered flight, so jealous she's near tears;
she wishes she could somehow join their games
through panes of wavy glass. She glumly peers
at birds she knows, though she can't say their names.

II

Until the favored one arrives, he'll wait;
for hours, he's hoped to see the yellow finch.
He has some chores, but he'll procrastinate
until the favored one arrives. He'll wait
to watch the golden greeting that his late
wife had so prized; he will not move an inch
until the favored one arrives. He'll wait
for hours; he hopes to see the yellow finch.

A Scarf for Her Father

She still remembers how she struggled, bent
over the needles that refused to hold
the loops she made, the fluffy yarn in bold
blue colors that she knew would complement
his eyes. She'd asked a lot from stitches meant
to heal a wound, to knit together old
untreated fractures, and to warm a cold
paternal shoulder. Oh, the hours she'd spent—
and what a mess she'd made, with one end wide,
the other narrow, full of holes and snags.
He never wore it. Weeks after he died,
she finds it in his closet, hung beside
his best blue tie: each day, those two blue flags
saluted him. At last, she's glad she tried.

The Patience of the Blue Ridge Mountains

I hadn't been back here for many years,
but I thought I recalled the smoky blue
and how the soft but solid ridge appears
to nudge the sky and calm its brighter hue,
a bulwark hovering protectively
above green fields and red barns, and dictating
how wind and sun will angle through each tree.
I've aged, of course—but while the ridge was waiting
for my return, it somehow hadn't crumbled
a bit. It hadn't faded or worn out
the way a memory can, nor had it stumbled
or sagged. Today it stunned me: strong and stout
as youth, blue-gray beyond my recollection,
and patient. It forgave me my defection.

Harbor Walk

Plymouth, Massachusetts

A hundred idle hulls bob in this bay,
nudged by the breeze and by a residue
of salty wanderlust, and while they stay

at anchor, I stride by, and wish I knew
the first thing about jib or boom or spar,
or how to tack across this ruffled blue.

I never learned to navigate by star
or wind or tide—but with each step I float
a little, and until I cross the bar,

this daily walk will take me to remote
new ports and home again. A restless mind
finds here both empathy and antidote:

these boats will sail again, they're not defined
by this hour of repose. Their intimation
of journeys promised lets me leave behind

well-traveled seas of heartache and frustration,
and charts my path along this sparkling bay
that lights and harbors my imagination.

Waiting for the Helicopter

The strangled slap of helicopter blades
awakens him from dreams of death to dreams
of rescue—and how readily he trades
apocalypse for Eden, ghosts for teams
of EMTs, this faithless forest for
a sky-hung promise. Yes, he will be saved;
tomorrow he'll enrich his hiker's lore
with tales of cold and hunger that he's braved.
His friends will be impressed; they'll buy him beers
and slap him on the back, as he pretends
he didn't ever feel these wrenching fears,
or wonder if this would be how it ends.
With aching head raised one inch from the ground,
he listens for salvation's whirring sound.

He listens for salvation's whirring sound—
the blessed beat of metal slicing air—
above his own half-strangled breath. He's found!
But is the helicopter really there?
He can't quite trust his ears; he can't quite feel
his toes; he blinks and blinks and still sees fog.
He wonders if his throbbing leg will heal,
or if death tripped him in that hidden log.
His water and his apples are long gone,
and as he licks his chapped and cracking lips,
he tries to taste a guarantee of dawn
beyond this hour when sun's bright solace dips.
He thinks it's been four days, or maybe five.
What's one more night? He's sure he can survive.

What's one more night? He's sure he can survive
the hunger and the cold and being lame
a little longer; help will soon arrive.
And then he hears a voice call out his name—
a distant, strangled sound like tuneless singing.
He'd answer, but he can't quite catch his breath,
and maybe it's his own ears he hears ringing,
or else, perhaps, the siren song of death.
He shakes himself, remembers bravery,
and makes some bargains. If he's rescued, then
he'll rescue others, and die gracefully
some other time. Adventure's great, but when
that big adventure comes, he'd rather die
at home. He'd plan a dignified goodbye.

At home, he'd plan a dignified goodbye.
He'd gather friends to share a gourmet meal:
roast lamb with new potatoes, key lime pie,
and good champagne (it's time to break that seal).
And then he'd crawl beneath some crisp, clean sheets,
recite a childhood prayer, and close his eyes
without the strangling fear that now defeats
his efforts to be stoic, calm, and wise.
But would he be so peaceful? Might he rage
at death despite some warning and some time?
Will he resist death even in old age,
as unprepared for it as in his prime?
Enough of dreams and dark philosophies—
he won't be rescued by his fantasies.

He won't be rescued by his fantasies,
but still his lungs fill up with so much hope
it nearly chokes him. Here among the trees
he's drowning, and he reaches for a rope.
Or is he falling? Will there be a net?
Or has he had a stroke? That would explain
this fuzziness, and how he could forget
what day it is. He starts to think the strain
will strangle his poor mind. Another nap
might help; he'll rest, then come up with a plan.
He'll take another look at his trail map,
and maybe walk a little, if he can.
But now he's just too tired. So instead,
he hikes through the terrain inside his head.

He hikes through the terrain inside his head,
traversing easily a mountain trail
whose grade and elevation cause no dread,
because he's positive that he won't fail.
The vista from the summit makes him gasp—
the light and color and sheer magnitude
more than a mortal should expect to grasp—
and maybe that's the point. This altitude
impairs his breath, and half-awake, he turns
to find another trail, another view,
but awe still strangles him, his chest still burns,
and he's still lying in the dirt. A few
bright stars beam down, each one a hopeful spark
insisting on itself despite the dark.

Insisting on itself despite the dark,
his confidence rebounds a little bit.
Believing optimism is a mark
of strength, he does his best to nurture it.
He thinks of home instead of hunger, day
instead of darkness, and that does the trick.
He'll get through this; he really feels okay,
although somewhat lightheaded and homesick.
He pulls his collar up around his chin,
then lifts his head, as if the stars have beckoned—
and thinks he sees a chopper's rotors spin
in shiny circles, brighter every second.
His strangled heartbeat mimics, as it fades,
the strangled slap of helicopter blades.

II
Songs of Travel

"Along the road to Anywhere,
the wide world at our feet . . ."
—Robert Service, "The Tramps"

Same Model and Year, Different Speed

In sputtering haste, my automotive twin
flies past me. While I dawdle down Route Three,
what makes him drive his rattle-trap of tin
in sputtering haste? My automotive twin
most likely carries dents and rust akin
to mine, but those are flaws that you can't flee
in sputtering haste. My automotive twin
flies past me while I dawdle down Route Three.

The Bourne Bridge, Late October

en route to Cape Cod

By now most visitors have left, and ceded
this bridge to locals; we drive unimpeded
in both directions, happy to be done
with summer's frantic pilgrims to the sun—
and yet the span unsettles me. It rises
along a modest pitch, but mesmerizes
and disconcerts me at this time of year.
As I approach, the apex seems too near,
the route across the water much too short,
so that I haven't got the time to sort
uneasiness and awe and satisfaction,
my brain about to take in just a fraction
of bird's-eye beauty as my lungs inhale
too little salty breeze. My eyes will fail
to fully grasp the blue above and blue
below, the red and orange that outdo
each other on the shore, the green of stoic
and sturdy pines, their constancy heroic
but humble. And I won't quite understand
the sinuous geometry of land
affectionately licked by water or
the physics of the delicate rapport
between steel beams and thin air. Though my wheels
grip asphalt firmly, I confess it feels
as if I might veer off into the sky
or fall into the water—learn to fly
or learn my limitations. I know some
who near this bridge are near their ends; they come
to jump, just past the sign that urges *Call*

Samaritans. But I drive on, through all
I can and can't absorb, what rattles me
and what makes this brief ride a partially
unopened gift. About two thousand feet
of pavement and the crossing is complete,
and every time, I reach the Cape before
I've thought of words for all I can't explore.

Reunion Sonnets

for Cam, Jane, Kate, Maureen, and Sally

I. Old South Carriage Tour

Charleston, South Carolina

The weary horse pulled six loud tourists through
the streets of Charleston, through a history
of war and earthquake, where magnolias grew
to lush and sturdy heights, as graciously
as if they'd witnessed only years of ease,
as if they'd found exactly what they'd needed
among these palms and wrought-iron balconies
and southern sun, and so they had succeeded.
We too had bloomed, each where she had been planted,
and all of us knew just what had been lost
and gained, in decades poor and prosperous.
The yearly sharing of our stories granted
a peace more dear because we knew the cost,
and history would never weary us.

II. Where Everybody Knows Your Name

Boston, Massachusetts

We'd known each other's names for decades; soon
we'd probably begin forgetting them.
But meanwhile, our accustomed stratagem
for staying young led us one afternoon
to Boston's Beacon Street, and a saloon
immortalized on TV screens as "Cheers,"
now luring tourists with expensive beers
and t-shirts. We believed the show's theme tune:
the one about ignoring worries, taking
a break with buddies where life's worst offenses
can't get to you, can't even make you flinch.
Because all troubles are the same, and slaking
your deepest thirsts brings you to your best senses,
we raised our glasses at the Bull and Finch.

III. Girls' Cruise

Western Caribbean

At Playa Uvas, Cozumel,
we kayaked, although not too well.
With greater expertise, we shopped,
and showed yet more skill as we hopped
from spa to bar to beach, then back
to bar. Tequila shots and Jack
and ginger had beguiling charms;
so did the barkeep's muscled arms.
We really liked repeating *sí*
and *uno más*, but finally,
we made our way back to the dock—
our ship would sail at ten o'clock.
When midnight brought the big buffet,
we all were fast asleep. *¡Olé!*

The Powell-Mason Cable Car

San Francisco, California

A roller coaster for sedater souls—
without the cerebellum-rattling speed,
without the screams—it climbs and dips and rolls
at stately tempos, limit guaranteed
by cable's crawl. The gripman clangs the news
of stops and starts, and you won't gasp with fear;
you'll merely gawk at dazzling downhill views
and inhale bay-enchanted atmosphere.
Hop on, and see a city that respects
its hills, a city built and then rebuilt
on steep grades where a fault line intersects
with fearlessness. Instinctively, you tilt
into the urban thrill ride's undulations,
a willing pawn of underground vibrations.

Driving to Key West

Coasting
along
Route One
from key
to key
to key,
feeling
lighter
with each
milepost,
we stop
often—
to swim,
explore,
stare at
endless
aqua
water,
eat pie
(Key Lime,
of course)—
in no
hurry
to reach
the road's
end.

Edward Hopper's Hotels

after three of his paintings

I. *Hotel Lobby*

Two women silently disrupt this space.
One wears a bright red dress and tilts her chin
up toward her dark-clad husband, in her face
the angles of a quarrel she will win.
The other reads her book, oblivious
to how her yellow hair affronts the gray
around her. They don't care, it's obvious,
that management might frown upon the way
their bared legs undermine the dim restraint
of shadows and straight lines, and neither one
is fazed by the imperious complaint
the husband seems to make. A slice of sun
slants through the door and toward the women's shoes,
an overture all three of them refuse.

II. *Hotel Room*

She has to leave this town, and right away.
Half-dressed, she checks the schedule: there's no train
tonight, and so until the light of day,
she's stuck here in a mess she can't explain.
At least this hotel room is halfway neat.
The bed on which she perches is half-made;
packed suitcases stand upright and discreet
beside the single armchair where she's laid
her dress; her shoes wait side by side; she's placed
her hat atop the bureau. But the room
is falsely tidy. What can't be erased
from vacant walls and pale limbs will consume
her half-hearted resolve unless she makes
her exit soon and unpacks her mistakes.

III. *Hotel by a Railroad*

The view outside his hotel window lacks
the slightest elegance; his indignation
stiffens his neck. But profit rides those tracks,
and so compulsory appreciation
prolongs his gaze. He thinks that if he stands
and stares and smokes, the pose might signal both
that he's no snob and that he still demands
the best. The truth is, he's confused, but loath
to show her that. She slouches in her slip,
head bent, observing nothing but her book.
She's tired of him; she's weary of this trip.
She knows that nothing here deserves a look—
not him of course: blank as these walls and closed
as bureau drawers, well-dressed and too well-posed.

Flying Companion

The man in 10B kneads his hands and closes
his eyes; his jaw line tenses as the plane
begins its desperate taxiing to gain
what speed it can. 10A already dozes,
but takeoff's test of buoyancy exposes
10B's anxiety. Arthritis pain
or circulation defects might explain
the kneading, but more likely it discloses
involuntary efforts to keep calm,
to rub out fear. I sense it from 10C:
although *hello* is nearly all we've said,
I feel the presence of another palm
as sweaty as my own. We tacitly
share perfectly companionable dread.

Passport Control

Charles de Gaulle Airport

"Control"? No, it was anarchy
as four lines funneled into three,
then two, all ending up inside
a maze of rope lines that defied
our hopes for just a modicum
of dignity. And then as someone poked me in the back, we heard,
from yards away, the latest word.
A uniformed official yelled,
so loudly that she'd have excelled
at drawing distant livestock near,
"All U.S. passports over here!"
Yes, in that crowded and chaotic
room—some of us near psychotic
with exhaustion and frustration—
we found new cause for irritation.
Although we'd heeded every sign,
we'd waited on the wrong damned line.

On the Spanish Coast

for Marcia, Terry, Steve, Ed, Heinrich, and Gregg

This little town looked out to sea,
and from our hilltop, so did we,
basking in rented ease. We'd get
to Barcelona—crowds and sweat
and Gaudi's gaudy majesty—

and at the mountain winery
we'd drink red, white, and history.
But each day when the sun had set,
this little town

would draw us back to reverie
on coastal heights. We earnestly
attempted basic etiquette
in Catalán, and locals met
us halfway—as if home might be
this little town.

The English and Their Queen

State Opening of Parliament, London

The Coldstream Guards play Elgar; golden braids
adorn the coats of horsemen on a route
that once bore kings whose rule was absolute,
and now this Queen for more than six decades.
This rite is old, but her crown never fades,
its splendor still sufficient to recruit
these regiments of riders, every boot
and buckle shining in precise parades.
The tourists gather, though a gray sky spits,
and locals, too, seem wide-eyed, just as ready
to see, through veils of rain, a regal glow.
Do they remember courage in the blitz?
Do they admire her posture, straight and steady
despite her age? Why do they love her so?

It hardly matters why they love her so.
One Englishman explains that they respect
her diligence, her promise to protect
their heritage. As P.M.'s come and go,
she stays, her subjects proud to rank below
her gray-haired eminence, so often decked
in someone else's jewels. You can't elect
your living history, star of this show.
Well, yes, but this is more than civic pride
or national nostalgia; pageantry
makes public a more visceral emotion.
Pale faces light up, and it seems I've spied
on private depths, bared inadvertently:
a rainless realm of reasonless devotion.

The Salisbury Crags

Edinburgh, Scotland

Along these crags, near Arthur's Seat,
you watch your own slow tourist feet
connect the dots of random stones,
sidestepping falls and broken bones.
Then you look up and see—complete—

an epic realm. Green hillsides meet
a gray stone castle; down the street,
a palace preens. A Forth wind moans
along these crags,

chastising those who fear defeat
by pebbly paths. Small perils greet
the hiker, while time's rigor hones
a city's pride: the thistle throne's
high heather nods, and lost hearts beat
along these crags.

Well Fed

The Amalfi Coast, Italy

Hungrier than we knew, we feasted here
on apricots and cherries and cheap wine,
then stretched our leaden limbs along these sheer
gray cliffs, adapting to their sinuous line.
The jasmine breath of earth infused our own
as new buds bloomed on ancient mountainsides,
and when the salt sea breached our veins of stone,
it challenged and re-charted human tides.
Anointed by the sun's benevolence
where banks of bougainvillea blazed untamed,
we too became a source of radiance,
reflecting blessings we could not have named.
Embraced by lemon-terraced hills, we flourished:
not merely sated, but profoundly nourished.

III
Sea Sonnets

"Wanting the sticky, salty sweetness
Of the strong wind and shattered spray . . ."
—Edna St. Vincent Millay, "Exiled"

Sunrise at Sea

for the KKL Krew

Out here, it's only sea and sky. Content
together in the boundless black of sleep,
they hardly heed the morning sun's ascent—
but pale persuasion's reach is wide and deep.
Across the atmosphere, a restless glow
disturbs unconscious ebony, each stream
of saffron, lilac, peach, and indigo
a variation on a waking dream.
Along the water, too, the nascent light
of day undoes the dark; as night's ink fades,
the waves awaken, raising wisps of white
that dapple drifting teal and turquoise shades.
Like lovers loath to rise when night is through,
both sea and sky stretch slowly into blue.

The Waves

Sprawled on a pew of sand, you meditate
on miracles of tide and time. Without
a prayer but apparently devout,
and humbled by the water's shifting weight,
you watch with wonder, even venerate
this higher power rolling in and out:
omnipotence too obvious to doubt,
authority too awful to debate.
Like salty spray, some blue-green grace may cling
and seep unsanctified into your soul,
without a psalm or sermon, for the sea
makes its own joyful noise. The breakers ring
uncounted changes, and no church bells toll
more faithfully or irresistibly.

Autumn Wish

I wish for seaside weightlessness once more
before I huddle in a heavy coat
and hide my hands in mittens, and before
I wind a woolen scarf around my throat.
I want the salt and sand to stick to me
as if I were a barnacle or bird,
as light as air and thriving thoughtlessly,
anxieties erased and debts deferred.
Unshod, unscheduled, and uninsulated,
I'd drop my shoulders and I'd lift my head,
my step as careless and uncalculated
as winds and waves by wanton currents led.
I want to walk this beach in weightless ease,
a summer girl once more before the freeze.

The Roaring

The wind pulled at his hair, the cold spray stung
his brow, the sand blew in his eyes—and this
felt just right for a fool like him, who'd flung
his last chance past the breakers. An abyss
as deep as any ocean soon would claim
what future he had left. He heard derision
in crashing waves that seemed to roar his name,
condemning him and his reckless decision.
Who knew the ocean would be so unkind,
would salt regrets, leave rages newly stirred?
Enough. He went home, left the sea behind,
and poured himself the liquid he preferred.
He drank some scotch, then shuffled off to bed,
but he still heard the roaring in his head.

My Grandmother and the Sea

My father's mother said the beach would make
her cry. Did she mean that the spray would sting
her eyes? Or would the timeless breakers bring
to mind old dreams, or some recurring ache?
My own eyes watch the waves and read my book
and sometimes close as I sit half-reclined,
my skin still smooth where hers was deeply lined;
I wonder what she saw. Perhaps she took
too hard the rude assault of '38,
when breakers broke into the Legion Hall;
perhaps the salty reach reminded all
her unshed tears of their collective weight.
Or else the place just made her heart too full—
like mine, a captive to the ocean's pull.

Woman and Small Boy at the Beach

She's not his aunt or babysitter; prone
to panic, they would hover, while instead
she keeps her distance, lets him rule his own
sandcastle kingdom, lets him run ahead—
but not too far. Although discreet, she's near
enough for rescue should the despot stumble,
or should aggressive seagulls make him fear
a coup d'état, or should a castle tumble.
She strikes a balance only mothers can:
despite her loose-limbed, hands-in-pockets bearing,
her sharp eyes nimbly sweep the sandy span
commanded by the object of her caring.
Her instincts keep him close enough, but free
to revel in his seaside sovereignty.

Memorial for Ben

in memory of Benedict Quinn Underhill (1959–2018)

Ben swam against the tide for many years,
and wrestled currents that he knew would take
his breath away. He spat out pain and fears,
and made more of his life than most men make.
And he made stalwart friends who now have come,
as he'd requested, to this chilly shore
where he grew up. They weep and hug, and some
tell stories; there's a toast, then one thing more
they do for Ben. They dive into the sea,
most laughing, each one with a fist clenched tight:
boys in their fifties—mourning, but with glee,
illuminated by the slanting light
of summer's end and braced against the cold
by love for him whose ashes they all hold.

Coastal Fog

The shoreline welcomes air the shade of tin:
a damp salute seeps upward from the sea
while drapes of mist descend to meet their kin,
as gray as gloom, murky as mystery—
but gladness gathers in suspended dew.
The coast wants clouds as children want the touch
of parents; elemental bonds as true
as blood connect the ocean with the much-
maligned moist atmosphere. And if you've seen
this inbred fog unfurl like sodden lace
that mutely mends the sunlit split between
the sea and sky, you've seen an old embrace.
Clear skies more brightly thread the seaside loom,
but ashen veils bring comforts of the womb.

When You Find Me Staring at the Ocean

Because you ask me what I'm looking for,
I tell you *nothing*—but that's not quite true.
I stare in this direction to restore
my sense of indirection; to see through
a sea of obligations, plans, and jobs;
to float instead of swim; to leave behind
the getting and the spending amid mobs
all headed in their own directions, blind
to all but their to-do lists, dutiful
and destined to dry out into cliché.
I've done that. Right now I'm responsible
for little more than breathing in the spray
from waves I watch. I know that if I stare,
I might find everything or nothing there.

IV
Shared History

"Shared joy is a double joy;
shared sorrow is half a sorrow."
—Swedish proverb

Five Poems for Westhampton Beach, New York

I. Gloria's

Although it's now an upscale bakery,
and even back then its red awnings claimed
that it was "Seeley's," it will always be
just "Gloria's" to us: a shop we named
for its proprietor, the gray-haired, glum
provider of our daily Wonder Bread
and wisdom. She sold milk, watch bands, and gum;
informed us who was drinking, who was dead;
glared at both *Newsday* and the *Daily News;*
and always stocked Pepto, Clark Bars, cheap toys,
toothpaste. She'd fill your bag and add her views
on traffic, tourists, and skateboarding boys.
Her store was dark and cramped; the whole place smelled
of old dust and opinions firmly held.

II. Six Corners School

My father was assigned, in World War II,
to be a lookout, watching from his school's
high windows with some other kids. Their view
was lofty, but soon they'd be viewed as fools.
For Dad sent a report of something flying
through our town's quiet skies. Was it a bomb,
a German parachute? The mortifying
truth, soon broadcast by school-wide intercom,
was that he'd seen a weather balloon—no threat,
one of our own. Years later, Mom became
a teacher at that school; she wouldn't get
to watch for bombs, and never earned Dad's fame.
By then they both were busy mediating
their children's wars—petty, but irritating.

III. Westhampton Free Library

in memory of Judge Harold Medina

In villages like ours, wealth sometimes lurks
behind tall hedges, unseen and unshared.
But funds for our July Fourth fireworks
came from a thoughtful local judge who paired
that gift of noisy summer celebration
with quieter, timeless philanthropy:
he made more than one sizable donation
for new wings on our public library.
We'd walk down there with Mom (she loved the place),
step into silence, and breathe atoms shed
by paper, ink, and readers, each bookcase
his gift. The judge admired, his obit said,
the odes of Horace; our own favorites waited
in rooms his generosity created.

IV. Luna's Pizza

Theirs may just be the worst of pizza pies—
with cheese like rubber and a greasy crust;
too much of their cuisine would jeopardize
your health, I'm sure. But their trade is robust,
most likely due to that highway location:
on your way home, it beckons, and once more
you fall for it, hungry anticipation
defeating your good judgment. And before
you've swallowed that first mouthful, you regret
the calories about to be ingested
and the impatience that made you forget
that stones would be more easily digested.
But it has fans. My brother still insists
the pizza's great—though his heartburn persists.

V. Sense of Direction

I grew up knowing *south* was toward the water:
the ocean, only one mile down the road,
drew me as if I were a mortal daughter
born to Poseidon, whose ancient code
of pulsing thunder signaled me. I heard
his summons, and of course I knew the way;
the sea's familiar magnetism stirred
my thirst and led me southward to the spray.
West was toward the city, poor pretender
to glory; *north* was thatched with scrubby pine;
east was island's end, a distant splendor;
south was our prize. I've had to redefine
geography: from where I live today,
the sea lies east—but I still know the way.

Mom and Dad and the Moon

"We went to see the moon." That's what they'd say
when they came back from one of their excursions
to our town beach. We kids would spend the day
on that same sand, in our childish diversions—

we body-surfed, played Frisbee, bared our skin
beneath the lethal sun—but they would go
well after dinner, and to our chagrin,
they went alone. They said they liked the glow

of moonlight. We preferred bonfires and s'mores
and how black air could leave us pleasantly
unsettled as we heard familiar roars
now voiced by waves that we could barely see.

It might be that our parents felt the same
half-scary sense of near-intoxication,
but all they ever mentioned was that claim
about their bent for lunar observation.

When they retired, they traveled—to Belize,
Berlin, and Bali, Nagano and Nome—
adventuring until weak eyes and knees
discouraged journeying so far from home.

I once asked which adventures were the best,
knowing that age might steal their stories soon.
They traded sheepish grins, and Dad confessed,
"Those evenings when we went to see the moon."

Mirror Nonet for Three Sisters

Bred from a versatile vine, we might
be Zinfandel, Merlot, Chablis:
one inherited the curls,
one the tidiness gene,
one the travel bug—
three vintages,
three glasses
filled with
love,
which can't
reconcile
sweet and dry, or
golden and reddish,
but which softens the tongue,
and cools the throat once inflamed
by cross words and competition,
and ripens all we took from the vine.

Ovillejo for My Brother

All wit and grace and hairy shins,
he wins
at Scrabble, golf, and basketball;
it all
comes easily to him. And when
again
we lose, he proves his acumen
by opting not to gloat. The prize
is our esteem; each time he tries,
he wins it all again.

Song of Ourselves

"Tell me why the stars do shine,
Tell me why the ivy twines,
Tell me why the sky's so blue,
And I will tell you just why I love you."
                    —song lyrics by Mitchell Parish

It was the two-part harmony
that drew us irresistibly:
the tuning to each other, meeting
in a sound, without competing.
Mom and Dad would start—a blend
of sweet and strong we could depend
upon—and then we kids joined in,
four unripe voices, pure but thin.
We'd never have confessed we cared
about the way the neatly paired
vibrations warmed our throats and hearts,
but when we split into two parts,
we joined in something bigger than
our bickering, and we began
to understand more than we knew,
more than we sang.
                    Time passed, we grew,
and we kept singing. Decades later—
voices stronger, burdens greater—
those of us still here still sing.
With absent voices echoing,
we do our best to tune to one
another as we've always done,
the low notes twining with the high
in harmony that tells us why.

Family Reunion Photo Taken on a Cruise Ship

Much later, we would recognize our last
hurrah: this moment, hanging on my wall.
Afloat, well-fed, we never guessed how fast
a wave like ours could curl its lip and fall.
The sunshine sparkled, and we had no trouble
reflecting it; twelve pairs of eyes were full
of ocean blue, and still blind to the bubble
that barely held our luck. The tide would pull
us under soon; some faces have grown pale,
and some are gone—dementia, death, divorce,
and chemotherapy filling our sail,
unlucky stars charting a darker course.
The photograph depicts the pleasure cruise
that was our lives, a portrait of old news.

Inheritance

in memory of Susan Kreiling Lawless (1952–2013)

It was, at first, my mother's mother's ring,
and then somehow it skipped a generation,
and was my sister's. Subtly shimmering,
it was a delicate, old-world creation
that I thought would have looked good on my hand:
three tiny diamond chips set in a small
etched-silver oblong on a golden band.
Although we laughed about it, I recall
my jealousy; that heirloom was the one
I'd coveted—a wish I didn't hide—
but her slim finger wore it well. In fun,
she said she'd leave it to me when she died.
I wear it every day now, and I guess
there's nothing that I've ever wanted less.

My Father's Voice

in memory of Robert Taylor Kreiling (1930–2015)

Sometimes it seemed as if his voice alone
fixed almost everything; authority
and wisdom sang in his rich baritone.

More crooning cello than boastful trombone,
its deep notes pulsed with warmth and empathy,
and none who heard it ever felt alone.

In speeches, meetings, even on the phone,
he could persuade his staunchest enemy
to hear the truth in his rich baritone.

It often rang with wit—jokes at his own
expense, bad puns, masterful parody,
sly riddles—and he never laughed alone.

It still commanded me when I was grown:
I counted on that sound to help me see,
I heard the truth in his rich baritone.

Untuned by illness, that voice learned to moan
in pain; it rasped and sighed with frailty.
I held his hand, and he was not alone
when death at last silenced his baritone.

On the Ferry Home

in memory of Mary Louise Lucas Kreiling (1927–2016)

I've crossed this water many times before,
and often on this vessel; I adjust
my footing as it sways away from shore,
and wait to hear its hull creak in a gust.
Despite its aging bulk, the ferry glides,
and eases me across, this time to grace—
beyond the mysteries the sea confides,
beyond our island home, beyond where place
is mapped or years are counted—for I carry
the dust of home itself, the dust of one
who was our loving, breathing sanctuary,
one whose last odyssey is nearly done.
She sails home on this ferry, and she'll sleep
in island soil, where grace and love will keep.

The Watchers

My sister watches as I play a game
of Scrabble. She of course no longer plays,
but looks on mutely from within a frame
where we both smile on one of her good days—
the kind of day that would become more rare—
before the rounds of hellish therapies
that soon would take her strength and curly hair,
though she'd still smile, right through those miseries.

My father watches as I grade a stack
of papers; he lived long enough to know
that though I love my job, I often lack
sufficient patience for this part. My slow,
unsteady progress would have baffled him.
In this old photo, he strides rapidly
past colleagues who applaud; he's tall and slim,
his shoulders broad with easy dignity.

My mother watches as I turn the pages
of books that made the *Times* best-seller list—
but I can't tell her which of them engages
my interest, which of them should not be missed.
I took this snapshot on my porch last year;
she holds a book, but looks up at me, grinning,
as if at eighty-eight she has no fear,
as if she thinks the fun is just beginning.

Sometimes I search their eyes for confirmation
that I'm not wrong, that they still watch and care,
that there's still an ongoing conversation
among us, and that in some sense we share

the games, the work, the stories. Sometimes grief
defeats me, and I know I'm only posing,
pretending that their poses bring relief
or can repair what breaks with each life's closing.

But mostly I don't search or analyze.
I just look at my dead, in four-by-six
framed photographs, and sometimes when my eyes
meet theirs, shared history performs its tricks:
my sister cheers my latest triple Q,
my father tells me that he's proud of me,
my mother says she liked that novel, too,
and love resists life's awful brevity.

About the Author

Jean L. Kreiling is the author of two previous collections of poetry, *Arts & Letters & Love* (2018) and *The Truth in Dissonance* (2014). Among the honors her work has earned are the *Able Muse* Write Prize, the Great Lakes Commonwealth of Letters Sonnet Prize, the Kelsay Books Metrical Poetry Prize, two Laureates' Prizes in the Maria W. Faust Sonnet Contest, three New England Poetry Club prizes, the Plymouth Poetry Contest prize, and the *String Poet* Prize. Kreiling is Professor Emeritus of Music at Bridgewater State University in Massachusetts, and she also taught English at Western Carolina University in North Carolina; her articles on the intersections between music and literature have been published in numerous academic journals. She is Associate Poetry Editor of *Able Muse Review: A Journal of Poetry, Prose & Art* and a longtime member of the Powow River Poets.

Made in United States
North Haven, CT
26 January 2022

15294436R00055